Things to Pack on the Way to Everywhere

poems

Grisel Yolanda Acosta

Praise for *Things to Pack on the Way to Everywhere*

Dr. Grisel Y. Acosta's poems, "dark and precise like *Borges Laberintos*" are acutely aware of their punk and piercing powers. Such poems shriek fearlessly in black-lipsticked memory, and shine in their freakish dancing where chicas must always be "fighting for the ownership of our lives." Here you will find poetry that insists on schooling readers about a distinct kind of education and memory in relation to the creation of Acosta's identity. Acosta's poetry insists her readers bring new eyes, new hands, new minds, new anthems, and new music that is necessary and marvelous for its own sake, for its own wounds, and its own dreaming of dark and light. One of Acosta's many strengths is her rich, un-bossed, and marvelous voice, which is always fierce, humorous, intelligent, and sensual. These fearless poems hold their own in the ring, unflinching and startling in their symphonic journey through the dangerous and complex fissures of family, race, womanhood, culture, blood, and belonging. Acosta places us at the defiant center of her art and her memory, which dazzles in its truths, powers, stars, feasts, scars, and songs. In this book, you will find that altars and bodies are inseparable, and you will discover a world where women's lives open and close like pairs of bold, dark eyes. Acosta declares, "My mother was dark, too, but she had no voice. Today, I am her voice."

–RACHEL ELIZA GRIFFITHS

"I would be tempted to say, 'Reader, go straight to "Textbook on the Desegregation of an Afro-Latinx" if you want to witness the birth of a decolonized poet,' but that would cheat you out of the surreal, dangerous, and mythologized journey that is *Things to Pack on the Way to Everywhere*. As soon as you enter Acosta's book, you are in the middle of a ritual, a dispatch from a poet who is on speaking terms with death. There is no travelling light in this orbital Afro-Latinx journey. Acosta time bends with precision and can take us to the exact moment where we understand the strength of our resistance to rote definitions of identity. This is punk poetry heavily invested in abolishment of oppressive tropes, a reading experience where board games become ideological battle grounds, where playground games become yet another portal into our mortality. To be sure, Acosta will make you laugh and cry on this trip while she riffs with Lauryn Hill, becomes a poet of the Americas, and makes you grateful for every waking breath you take."

—WILLIE PERDOMO, *The Crazy Bunch*.

Open to any page in this book and the musicality of Grisel Acosta's language jumps out at you. Her words dance to a multitude of beats, be it hip-hop, hard rock, salsa or rhythm and blues. Like her eclectic musical influences, the subject matter and structures of Acosta's poems are enthrallingly diverse. Her innate intelligence, sense of personhood and social consciousness shine through on virtually every page. This book is well packed, literally and figuratively for a journey that will take the reader most everywhere. I know you'll enjoy the ride. Bon Voyage!

—DANNY SHOT, author of *Works* (CavanKerry Press, 2018); Associate Poetry Editor at Tribes.org

In *Things to Pack on the Way to Everywhere*, Grisel Y. Acosta uses language like a two sided coin, constantly hurling it in the air and watching it as it lands: a door - toss the coin - it lands - there is no door - toss the coin - it lands - Pelibre - toss it - it lands - the American Dream. Acosta constantly reminds us what women are expected to give up for small freedoms, for love, how our silence will kill us, "so you better learn to yell and cuss and spit the evil eye." Her world is one of music and punk sensibility. She is boisterous, and inquisitive, she is challenging and precise. Her many sides rattle us: dream weaver, music archivist, child of the diaspora — this work, these poems are a refreshingly and indispensable voice in the poetry of the Americas.

—**YESENIA MONTILLA**, author of *The Pink Box* (Willow Books, 2015) &

Muse Found in a Colonized Body (Forthcoming from Four Way Books, 2022)

Dedicated to Vincent Toro

Get Fresh Books Publishing, A NonProfit Corp.
PO BOX 901
Union, New Jersey 07083

www.gfbpublishing.org

ISBN: 978-1-734-5802-5-9
Library of Congress Control Number: 2021932596

Cover image by Grisel Yolanda Acosta
Cover design & book layout: Sara Pinsonault

Acknowledgements

"Beneath the Ivy" and "The Lamentation of Argon" were previously published in *Red Fez*.

"Chicago DJ Remix, North and Damen, 1993" was previously published in *Acentos Review*.

"Concentric Circles" was previously published in *MiPoesias American Cuban Issue*.

"Dream Water Breath Death" was previously published in *El Mundo Zurdo: Selected Works from the Meetings of the Society for the Study of Gloria Anzaldúa 2007 & 2009*, *Güeras y Prietas: Celebrating 20 Years of Borderlands/La Frontera*, and *MiPoesias American Cuban Issue*.

"The ENCRoach Program" has been accepted to the *Latinx Archive's Speculative Fiction for Dreamers*, to be published in 2021.

"Freelancing (The Truth about Contingent Labor)" was previously published as "Freelancing" in *Love You Madly: Poetry about Jazz*.

"Hardcore Chica Punk Birth Fragments" was previously published in *In Full Color: The First Five Years Anthology* and *Short Plays on Reproductive Freedom: 34 Short Plays and Performance Pieces from the Reproductive Freedom Festival and Words of Choice*.

"Hard Rock (The Truth about Jezebel)" was previously published in *Celebrating Twenty Years of Black Girlhood: The Lauryn Hill Reader*.

"Invisible Ink" was part of Black and White Bar's *Fahrenheit Around the World* Online Reading, May 3, 2020.

"It Takes a Pandemic" is my published contribution to the ongoing group poem by the same name, sponsored by City Lore and Bowery Arts + Science, which was inspired by Roni Schotter.

"Mother, Father, Child of the Americas" was previously published in *Chicana/Latina Studies: The Journal of Mujeres Activas en Letras y Cambio Social*.

"Nothing But Us" was previously published in *Celebrating Twenty Years of Black Girlhood: The Lauryn Hill Reader*.

"Pelibre Latinx" was previously published in *The Paterson Literary Review*, Issue 45.

"Pelota de Fuego" was previously published in *The Paterson Literary Review*, Issue 45.

"Revolution Mami" was previously published in *Celebrating Twenty Years of Black Girlhood: The Lauryn Hill Reader*.

"Textbook on the Desegregation of an Afro-Latinx" was previously published in *American Studies*.

"The Aliens" was previously published in *Pembroke Magazine*.

"The Guts of a Corporation" was previously published in *Kweli Journal*.

"Trash" was previously published in *Tattoosday Online Journal* and *The San Antonio Express News*.

"Ways of Seeing My Brothers" was previously published, in a slightly different version, in *The Best American Poetry* blog.

"We are Not All in the Same Quarantine" was previously published by *A Gathering of the Tribes* as part of its Tribes Virtual Open Mic: A Gathering in the Time of Covid-19.

"We Carry the Earth" was commissioned by the Lights for Liberty Vigil in Leonia, New Jersey; the poem was previously published by *The Baffler* and by *Split this Rock*.

Contents

...the first steps...

We Carry the Earth

We bring the harvest and lay it at an altar
of bread crust, pierced gold earrings, and the bones of our first born

Banana leaves halo the foundation of her body,
we salt the sand she rests upon, sprinkling the mineral from seashells

We pick translucent grapes and squeeze the juice into our downturned
mouths, lay gardenias to frame her death, perfume the pain within our muscles

You see a carcass of stone, barren of life, bleached ossein,
we see the child that ran between the Saguaros and wore red Matucana's in her hair

Cognac woven leather wrapped her brave feet as her toes tipped
sharp rock, skipped over puddles bordering the desert on lucky rain days

White sun burned through camisas de primos, sent to us del Norte,
worn threads unraveling with each day of wear, cada dia without descanso or certainty

Black hair flying like whipping palms, set aflight from much needed breezes
cooled café skin burning cedar brown with each step on the red tawny dirt taking us closer

Cyan sky hovered over our contorted path, twisted like a sapphire river
pooling into a sea of compadres singing the blues at the frontera, asking,
"¿Y de donde tu vienes?"

It must have been the cold
concrete holding her like iron gate
choking her lungs into frozen
prayer, holding her breath
tight within grey mucus and swollen sacs
bubbles of air that stopped
circulating, like language,
words that fall dead on icy ears.

mihcacocone
tlahquilli
tlamiz †

Se murio de neumonía.
There was no water.
There was no soap.
I was taken away from her.
Lloró en la mañana.
She called to me at 3 am.
I was not there.
You were not there.
We were not there.
We still are not there.
She will continue to cry her song in wind until we are there.
A shriek in the current is free to move, cross, fly beyond the flimsy delusion of barriers.

Her body will dust your land which is my land which is our land
We do not carry danger to your door
There is no door
There is no danger
There is only land
There is only earth
We carry this Earth on our skin
We carry it in our lungs
We carry it as our body which holds all bodies
Dirt from many tierras that are one tierra
We set it at an altar
We set you at the altar
We set ourselves at the altar
We set our firstborn at the altar
See the altar
See the Earth
Come carry it with us
Carry the child
Carry the family
Carry the people who are your people who are yourselves
You have been invited.

† *The words at the center of the poem are in the Nahuatl language. They mean "dead children,"*
"tomb," and "this will end."

The Astronomical Vision of the Tairona Kogi...

...entered my kitchen when I was 10 years old
                          mid-discussion with my brother Luis, regarding the 1st space
              shuttle flight—my abuela, Papi's mother, happened to be visiting, and she listened
                          as he explained our Earth's orbit 'round the fire of the sun

                    my grandmother became antsy, not her usual cool self
interjected a description of the cosmos that envisioned the Earth as zenith
                          hurling stars around us, their center point, a shell surrounding it all

        I felt embarrassed for my grandmother
              a woman known for her fierce wisdom
                          how could she make this mistake? I thought
        Lou later whispered, "she doesn't have an education"

it took me 25 years of schooling to dis/re/un-cover
              abuela's cosmology, rooted in the vision of the Tairona, illustrated
              as an egg by the Kogi

              for a moment, I felt embarrassed at my early assumptions
        wished I could go back and ask better questions, but now
                    I realize, abuela knew educating her son, my Papi, meant
                          educating his daughter and
                          educating whomever else I may encounter

Hardcore Chica Punk Birth Fragments

When someone says, "Latina," you get images of Salma Hayek, J-Lo, nowadays maybe even a graceful, ballet-trained Zoe Saldaña. You think of food and salsa dancing and accents, and no binge-watching time spent with April Ludgate on *Parks and Rec* can erase that indelible image. But we aren't all piñatas and mangos, for freak's sake. We are dark and precise like Borges' *Laberintos*, nerdy and cold like our Russian brethren who left us their names, bizarre and vicious like Al Jourgenson, el Cubano himself.

> *"Research has clearly demonstrated higher rates of maternal and infant*
> *mortality in African American, Latina, and Native American families."*

My mother was dark, too, but she had no voice. Today, I am her voice. It goes beyond my tattoos and piercings. See, Mami had two boys; enough for her, she thought. No one bothered to tell my mother that she had to remove the IUD after a certain amount of time, so when several years had passed and she found herself pregnant with me, she was surprised. I grew in her belly despite the big murderous piece of plastic that was my roommate. My tiny limbs grew in a hostile environment in order to give my mother what she always wanted: a girl.

> *"Latina women have higher rates of congenital*
> *abnormalities in their infants than other women."*

She asked to not be sedated so that she could see my birth, but the doctors lied to her and conked her out anyway. Apparently, doctors at Mercy Hospital in Chicago don't give a shit about Cuban mothers, or their uteruses, or their daughters growing in their bellies, or their wishes, or simple pieces of information that can make them happy, or saving their lives, or saving their daughter's lives. Mami accepted the disrespect silently.

> *"Poverty, discrimination and gender all impact socioeconomic status. Lack of*
> *resources leads to barriers to obtaining and maintaining care for all groups."*

I was loud. And I fought. I fought to live in her womb, and then be born, and only a few months later, during the Christmas and New Year holiday, I fought to live despite becoming sick with pneumonia. My father sat in the hospital with me as I cried and cried in pain from within a crib encased in plastic. He could only insert his hand through a rubber glove to touch me and I grabbed his thumb and, according to the story he always tells, I did not want to let go. The hospital did not allow him or my mother to stay with me overnight.

They hated to leave me, but I survived. By the time I was four months old, I had kicked death's ass twice. I was *born* a punk.

"The United States, for all its resources, should not have the highest rate of infant mortality amongst the 27 wealthiest countries in the world."

One year, when I was not 10 years old yet, I dressed up as a punk for Halloween. I wore a trash bag as a dress and cinched it with my mom's wide purple fabric belt with the rhinestone buckle. I got the idea from European music videos on the MV3 channel, videos about chauffeurs (Duran Duran) and cannibals (Shriekback). My afro was sprayed with orange and pink hair color, my lipstick was black, and my eyes were outlined in silver. The picture Tía took of me, in the room we shared, was full-length; I stood with my hand on my hip, head cocked to one side and the attitude on my face was *deadly*...and pretty silly.

The next year, I was the ghost of a motorcycle biker who had a terrible accident. I wore jeans and a jacket, a raggedy white T-shirt, a pull-on mask that was gruesome, a denim hat and knee-high boots. Papi kept asking what I was because he didn't understand my costume and it made me furious that I had to keep telling him. Deep down, I was furious because he would have understood a Miss Universe costume better. Was he even different than the men who sedated Mami?

"Inherent bias and systemic protocols both impact the ability of clinicians to care for all families equally."

But that's okay. I know. Even Miss Universe herself—who's almost always Latina—knows that under the sequins and paint, we are hardcore chicas, always taking advantage of your underestimation, always fighting for ownership of our bodies, ownership of our lives.

This poem quotes the "National Perinatal Association Position Statement, March, 2019: Perinatal Health Care Access and Disparities."

Concentric Circles

My Colombian cousins ask for Vuarnet
sunglasses and Girbaud jeans.
My parents cannot afford these gifts.
Huge photo portraits of Dorquitas and Angie
grace the high-ceilinged sitting room in Barranquilla.
I am jealous.
When I ask the fuzzy-haired maid for candy,
she expects some money.
"Noooo!" is all I can answer at 4 years of age;
the embarrassment I feel has no words.
No one has explained this dynamic to me.

Logan Square is a tough mix
of Cuban, Puerto Rican, Polish and Chinese
food, music, lacquered cars and glitter nails.
By sixth grade, we've learned blue eyeliner
looks best when it's running.
I hide my fear.
When the third-run movie theater boy
asks to rap* to me
the answer is yes.
One older girl laughs, watches, and inspects our moves,
unlike the big brother usher who is worried for all of us.

A white man decides my math
skills are better than what others thought.
Honors algebra will be the new home I
cannot speak of to my neighborhood
friends. They wouldn't get it.
I love the idea of variables.
A year later, geometry puzzles me.
Memorization of theorems is impossible.
The planes are visible,
they take shape among stars in space,
but my theory is different.

*To rap is slang for *kiss*.

10

Life on the Playground

after Ernesto Quiñones

if you walked by the lot that day
you might have assumed a child was saving a child's
life, body held tightly within another

girl's arms, possibly doing the Heimlich
she told us all it was like going to sleep
we trusted her because she was three years older: 11

the instructions were simple enough: breathe
deeply, huffing and puffing quickly, many times
her job was to press against our chests, tight, then—

poof—we'd be gone, out, as onlookers marveled
Pentecostal kids screamed it was evil, but we were daredevils
volunteered for the jump into oblivion, the escape

to somewhere beyond the smell of stale milk and oranges,
sweat and asbestos, rusted swings and old tar asphalt
teachers who didn't notice when we punched each other

I remember looking up to a circle of unknown kids, inspecting
my face, waiting for my eyes to open, wondering if
I would be the one who didn't wake up

Midwest Celebration

after Roxane Gay's "Black in Middle America"

You are 20 years old and want to get away to a nice place with your boyfriend. *The Chicago Tribune* has a travel section that advertises a bed and breakfast in Door County, Wisconsin, home of The Cherry Festival, and even though it is clearly corny, you think it is the perfect sweet thing to do. Cherry pies, cherry rice, cherry syrup, cherry drinks—and, of course, lots of antique shopping. You cannot afford furniture, but you have a beautiful collection of old glass in your bathroom window. Your boyfriend genuinely wants to make you happy and he borrows his father's big maroon truck you have to climb up into. The drive up is spectacular pre-fall crisp air and slightly turned green and gold leaves. Both of you sing along to Aerosmith's "Train Kept A-Rollin'" as you rest your feet on the dashboard and let the wind from the open window lift your hair like flames. The gravelly curve up to the inn has really big gnomes which make you laugh, but the innkeepers are polite and the room is big and a very happy yellow. It is just about dinner time and, apparently, the thing to do is go to a fish fry, as there are signs for such an event at nearly every restaurant. You pick one and watch the fire surrounding a huge black pot explode with the drop of the fish and then eat your meal surrounded by chubby, middle aged folks in L.L. Bean khakis. That evening, both of you giggle in bed.

The next day, the skimpy continental breakfast next to the gnomes in the yard leaves your stomach yearning for more. There are many cafés, so you drive to one of them and are seated at a nice table. Both of you talk about your plans for the day: looking at the cute shops, maybe bringing some jam back for the parents, going to the antique car show. The menu looks great and you are looking forward to some nice, fluffy pancakes, just like Mami made during summer vacations. Your boyfriend laughs at your grumbling stomach and both of you complain a bit about the lame breakfast that was advertised by the gnome inn but agree that the price of the B&B was still good. You look around the restaurant and see that everyone is eating except you. You notice that there are people who came in after you who are eating. You do not exactly believe what you are seeing and ask your boyfriend if the couple by the window came in after you did and he gives his polite smile and says, in a knowing tone, "Yes, yes they did." You wonder what to do and ask your boyfriend what to do and he says there is nothing you can do. You still wonder if this is a mistake and decide to go up to the counter—a walk which feels simple at first but then seems to take longer with each step—and mention to the person there that you have not had your order taken. The person does not look at you and says that a waitress will take your order soon. She does materialize after another 10 minutes and you order your food and continue to wait for it and are sort of but not really starving when the hotcakes arrive. You eat your pancakes, every bite, even though you know they are probably spit pancakes, even though you are no longer hungry. You still leave a tip when you are finished. You still go to look for glass. You still try to talk to the older woman in the antique store about red glass and why it is so rare but she refuses to answer you but instead of backing down you ask louder and she answers something about Depression glass without looking at you. You begin to count how many people of color you see.

Zero; even at the car show. You still bring home a bag of cherry rice for Mami, rice which she will never cook. You still show off your pictures to your friends at work and say the trip was really cute, even though you didn't celebrate with any cherry pie.

Hard Rock (The Truth about Jezebel)
(a song to sing for all young women in black kick 'em all boots)
after Lauryn Hill's "Doo Wop (That Thing)"

spike chains blue hair bad brains scream
identity issues broken mirror explanations
bring back black answers across oceans and seas
Caribbean music movements in screeching wails and bangs

hard rock girls shave their heads
hard rock girls have armpit hair
hard rock women aren't sanitary
hard rock women are diamonds, diamonds, diamonds

what are you afraid of?
warnings are futile

poseur punks in lime green and pink pathetic
money hungry corporate mimicry globalized murder
black boot bangs against fascist rhythms,
sexist clichés, racist schisms, yama, yama, yama, yama, yama, yama*

hard rock girls shave their heads
hard rock girls have fuzzy leg hair
hard rock women don't fear sexuality
hard rock women are diamonds, diamonds, diamonds

what the heck are you warning me of?

demolish machista demolition with angular philosophy
and androgynous gardens of soul crooning hula hoops
breast bearing bustiers and day-glo body paint piercing skank dance
tattooed serpent siren making rulers into followers with a baritone wink

hard rock girls shave their heads
hard rock girls have fuzzy hair
hard rock women wear oversized suits
hard rock women are diamonds, diamonds, diamonds

what are you afraid of?
warnings are futile

base base base saxophone drum beat beat beat
tough skin consciousness ready to defend against
ignorant don't know my history or your contribution
blindness red hair anger flows free in the pit, smiling, wild

hard rock girls shave their heads
hard rock girls have manic panic hair
hard rock women are educated mo-fos
hard rock women are diamonds, diamonds, diamonds

what the heck are you warning me of?
better beware of me
watch out
better beware of me
watch out
better beware of me
watch out
punk rock hard rock afro-woman diamond, diamond, diamond

*The word "yama" refers to "right living" and is used by the Afro-punk band X-Ray Spex in the song "Cliché."

...along the path...

Games

I refuse to play chess

        memorizing the paths of others for the purpose of conquering

anathema to me   I've cried more than once   playing

Monopoly, traumatized by my friends'

        bankruptcies, asking, "Why

        isn't the goal equal distribution?"

they call life a game
refer to the cliché "the cards one is dealt" in the same
breath as words like privilege
        urban
        social
        justice
associating humane behavior with our response to Las Vegas-oriented addictions

it was a gamble, going to the UIC English Department Chair who played
a game of golf in his long office, minutes before requiring I take every single English class
including developmental English; I was a graduate student
I will not pay off that debt until I am over 60 years old

at the Modern Language Association,
Reacting to the Past is the name of the game
we play, reliving the French Revolution; using dice
we rabble rouse and release armies, I ask "Why
are Lafayette and King Louis the only ones
rolling our fate? Why only the elite?"

        the leaders of the game do not answer my question

Nothing but Us
after Lauryn Hill's "Nothing Even Matters"

we're like the García Marquez couple
in *100 Years*, bound together in bed
reading Spanglish on each other's backs
palabras woven like warm quilt of Afro-
Diaspora, we ignore the outside world of mayhem and fallen tower chaos

my leg stubble mimics the brush on your face
combing the deep black sand of my body
the only chains here are our ancestors' bones, linked
we embrace candle wax lullabies lighting
our irises, flowers open and close and open and close

like breathing, your warmth moist in my lungs
I howl at 3 a.m. to stars that burst under eyelids
you echo with ocean song of salt and seaweed
we don't care that the mail has formed a ski slope
words avalanche onto peach lemonade porch sun-

set, resting without shame, let the job wonder why
we have abandoned paperwork and bureaucracy, free-
time is the ultimate goal of the indentured
I find centuries in your face, hieroglyphs
scrolled under your tongue when you say, "forever"

this moment will and will not end, depending
on the immovable mountain of dewy violets
we gather and snuggle atop of, turning pink and purple
ourselves with blood surfacing under brown skin, hot
and laughing at any notion of what might wither

Freelancing (The Truth about Contingent Labor)
after James Blood Ulmer's "Freelancing"

we are vines
reaching for the solid wall

    twisting around wrought iron
    a centrifuge spiraling dizzy

        grasping metal with teeth
        pointed and shiny hope

            pain hangs like unripe grapes
            light and bitter, unseen between spring leaves

        we crawl on the ground
        wanting more, hungry for life like an empty cave

    our green desire will smother beauty
    all over rotting stucco, old façades

and when our cloak of writhing madness
obscures the crumbling institutions

    then, will we bear our honey
    fruit, tasting of death and miracles

        a metallic surf scream
        the hesitancy of an embrace
            resting twilight on furrowed brick

Revolution Mami
after Lauryn Hill's "To Zion"

when I invited Mami to a restaurant dinner with activists
they ignored her, left her sitting quietly with her soup

stirred, boiled anger in me—didn't they know, or know to ask, what she did?
bravery isn't conferences and panels and books

Mami, in college, read every day alone in her bed, wasn't very social except
when she met Papi, who noticed, "She didn't talk much, but when she did, it was brilliant"

Papi went to my grandfather's flimsy wooden Cuban shack, asked for Mami's hand
Abuelo denied the marriage, said, "Tu eres muy Negro"

Mami married Papi anyway, didn't speak to Abuelo for 20 years
she lived in Barranquilla, the Colombian jungle, Princeton, and then Chicago with Papi

a photo of her, when I was born, has her looking away from the camera despite
the huge smiles on my father's and brother's faces, as if they don't see what she gave up, created

la guitarra is what brought her back to the world, me, her kinky-haired Afro-child
Santana, La Sonora Matancera, Paco de Lucía, "Piel Canela"

cinnamon skin, the soaked wooden curves of sound she
listened to on her bed on Saturday mornings while I read her books in Spanish

the child she was unafraid to give birth to, representation of love
of a Black man who fell in love with her mind, the sound of her voice

Mami, rubbing Vicks on my chest at 4 a.m.
Mami, making me eggs for dinner when I didn't want red meat
Mami, spending too much money on my classic Hollywood prom dress
Mami, singing the music of West Africa, Spain, Cuba, in her ramshackle Logan Square bedroom
Mami, giving up family to create new family, revolution family, revolution love (and Papi not
seeing what she sacrificed because she lived to give, like a singer gives until the voice is gone)
Mami, ignored by fashion revolutionaries who see her as just an old lady who hasn't done much
Mami, the one who embraced the Blackness in her, in her husband, in her daughter because
she knew her love was the only flag that matters, the only country without borders or castes

Suburban Cavewoman
(a song to sing when the road leads to outdoorsy types who have white supremacist tendencies)

I got DEET in my bloodstream
yeah, yeah
I got DEET in my blood stream
yeah, yeah

look at me, I'm a cavewoman
so tough
I eat bark and throw rocks
and wrassle stuff

I got DEET in my bloodstream
yeah, yeah
I got DEET in my blood stream
yeah, yeah

I climb big mountains
and break and blister myself
then let mommy and daddy pay my insurance
so I ain't worried about my health

I got DEET in my bloodstream
yeah, yeah
I got DEET in my blood stream
yeah, yeah

I've been pictured in
National Geographic for my feats
I can mimic animal sounds
I'm the master of chirps and bleats

I got DEET in my bloodstream
yeah, yeah
I got DEET in my blood stream
yeah, yeah

I've swum with the dolphins
and tackled hungry crocodiles
they've made documentaries of my life
but they're low budget and only for true cinephiles

I got DEET in my bloodstream
yeah, yeah
I got DEET in my blood stream
yeah, yeah

no one in the world is fiercer
than me
I got a contract with Animal Planet
so my friends can watch my wild life on TV

I got DEET in my bloodstream
yeah, yeah
I got DEET in my blood stream
yeah, yeah

I know my time is limited
next up is living with the bears
I'm pretty sure I'll be their dinner
but I'm pretentious so I guess that's only fair

I got DEET in my bloodstream
yeah, yeah
I got DEET in my blood stream
yeah, yeah

The ENCRoach Program

tinier water bugs and crickets make fun of me
my slavery, my burden
metal on my back, nearly half my weight
the death of me, looming
cracked exoskeleton under encrypted data

but they're next
I heard them, and that's my job
they said they'd make smaller chips
for smaller bugs' backs
little loads for all of us to carry

I thought, why not give back,
work for the community that feeds me
instead it's a betrayal of the poor
suckers who have the dirty neighborhoods
where I'm usually at, scrounging around
the tenements for an unnoticed crumb

what's to listen to? lovers, despair, hours of TV—dull!
so we got together, the roaches, the vermin
kept the mics on the abusers who attached the radios,
themselves, to us; the masters,
those who invented the chemicals that used to kill
us, those who would use us

now, to supposedly save the troubled,
those buried under rubble, the victims of natural disasters
they do not see that we are buried under their desires
our backs become thinner under cadmium, gold, silver, zinc,
and their words: "It has the potential for being
a redundant communication system at a low cost"

military men and university scholars
have many words to record; I've heard them all
like "$850,000 from the U.S. Army"
and "these are real bugs that can do bugging"
and "I always thought roaches were icky, but these are really cute"

my enslavement, the anvil on my back
forcing me to steal words from the same population I steal food from
never asking me if I wanted to move up to a federal offense
it is a curse, a forced vigilantism

we, the roaches of the world, once fed freely
conducted our business unfettered
now we must listen to our victims
hear them say, "Can we make the rent this month?"
while well-rested men listen on their computers
and the record is on our backs

This poem quotes sections of "Cockroaches Equipped as Wireless Networks," by Olga Kharif.

Mother, Father, Child of the Americas

It is raining in Can Serrat, orange
fruit in the trees outside my window drips
sugar into the cracks of blue tiles below,
a mosaic with words like *Yoko Ono* and *Electric Boogie*.
So, when my friend Nova, says, "Have fun in the Fatherland,"
equating Spain with dad-like things—order,
tweed jackets, or shaving tools lined on a towel—this father
seems incongruent with the motherly oil-scented water on my window.

We've just come back from Montserrat, la phenomenal
mountain range with impossible trails and religious artifacts.
We artists talk of the Spanish conquest, painfully
attempt to reconcile the blood-moistened soils of the Americas,
the mixture that made the bricks of the monastery the monks hoped would raise them up to God.
How could our mother, España, treat us so cruelly? Selfish
luxury abounds on the streets of Barcelona, gold rococo, surrealist curves in glass,
decadence we, too, now enjoy, at the price of ancestral slaves.

Or, maybe, no. Perhaps, this country of cured meats and wines isn't our mother, but
is our child, the true child of the Americas, a baby wrapped in blue seas and marble cathedrals.
We fed it guavas and corn, nursed it into cheerful peace to the rhythms of the Amazon,
let it suckle on the breast of rainstorms and coconut milk. We love our child,
combed its hair with translucent shells and dusted its face with sand-powder. We
spun its clothes with the sparkling salt of our oceans and our jaguar taught it
pride and fierceness. Oh, yes, she is our child, and we raised her well,
neglecting our own needs, letting our lands wither, get dusty with wrinkles and exhaustion.

I know this is true because I have seen how my own mother has given herself
to the point of neglect, letting her daughter shine in fancy dresses and degrees.
Who gets the credit for familial sacrifice? The fanciful child, so pretty in satin, or
la madre que sacrifica su último kilo para que su hija tenga lo mejor del mundo?
We want both the sacrificial mother and the spoiled child. Don't we? Both
the plain nun who forgives all our sins, the princess garbed in "borrowed" jewels and a sly wink.
Oh, to have for one day the Americas in cloaks of royalty! But she'd never.
She is la monja who gives and gives and gives so that all will fall in love with her hija,
the bitch who never feels guilty about wearing the diamonds of conflict.

White Latinx

after Jennine Capó Crucet

Imagine that you have not passed
when whitefolk align their TNT missiles at "Mexicans,"
meaning all perceived alien invaders, that they
know exactly who you are, what you eat for dinner.
The missives aren't because they feel to be at home, no,
these slurs are a whip, a lasso herding the cattle in
their presence, lest they stray too far.

Dream Water Breath Death

She rests on a beach she is not allowed on. Her clothes are from a store she cannot afford. In her dreams she wakes up to a house that is larger on the inside than it is on the outside. The flies have turned into water lilies that flap like fans to cool the midday death sun. The family dog takes her on a tour of the church spires that Gaudi-twirl into the depths of the inner labyrinth. Books line the walls of the room at the end of the spiral darkness that illuminates the words she never sees. Brown stained carvings reach to her and guide her into the main hall escalator where students ignore her arrival. She gets lost looking for her locker which has a combination she cannot remember. Her platform shoes were not given to her so she walks barefoot in golden sandals. Red candles mimic the blood on her hands which belongs to the mother she did not murder. The bicycle she wished for is not hanging on the back stairs that she repeatedly walks down while holding a knife. She is in the room she cannot find again and the students appear and reappear. If she crawls out of the knick knack nook she will be in her house again which she is already inside of. Her mother buys cheap ornaments that are expensive. The house is transparent to sunlight when she crawls into the darkness of the church spires and book room and the modern school. The larger rooms are within the walls which are skinnier than she is because not even the walls have eaten. She smiles her sadness with closed lips to hide the cosmetic dentistry that hasn't been done. Her cousin doesn't send letters that she reads closely to connect with the outside world. Water fills the school and she underwater paddles through the columns and arches and banisters. When she wakes up she is in the ocean that is not hers and swims with dreams that salt the world inside her walls.

The Lamentation of Argon*

you expect my spectrum of furor
to be directed at he who sizzles light in one dimension
the flat mist that turns night into deadly mercury ink

I could badmouth the orange specter
fling yellow mud like the child at summer's end
burn words in hollow tunnels that turn upon themselves

but why, when it is *you* who ignores my wavelengths?

ultraviolet blue sparkles skin at dusk

                                    my work!

electrons fizzle my spirit into deep magenta

                                    I did that!

viridescent clouds flash your currency on the corner

                                    me again!

yet you call me
yet you call *me*
neon
homeboy is one note: red and only red

I am multi-hued and constant
you call this lazy, inactive
name me slow poke
yet I shelter your instability in a bubble of protection
oxidation can't touch me
argon don't crack
this historian preserves your libraries, even
your drunken elixirs, all under rainbow lights

damn neon!
taking credit for it all
red-faced demon

I suppose it is only natural,
gas-like behavior to become enflamed

when one is limited to glass chambers: I don't blame neon

I blame those who see my work and call it neon
the way one might look at Earth and then call *all* planets Earth
oblivious to the scope of my charge

Argon is actually responsible for the entire rainbow of "neon" hues, other than red. Neon gas only produces red, yet is incorrectly named as the producer of all colors. Argon is also incredibly stable and is used in the preservation of food, historical documents, and wine.

Slick Product
(a song to sing when the world wishes to simplify the complexities of life)

Can you...
        make an audience roar, just like that?
        leave them begging for more,
        at the drop of your hat?
Do you
        have street men and scholars
        in your hip pocket?
Do you
        act like God...
        ...was in your momma's locket?

Are you a slick product
I can sink my chomps in?
Do you perform with intensity?
Are you a slick product
I can sink my chomps in?
Do you make thinkin' easy for me?

Do they
        all agree
        your words are impressive?
Do they
        take notes as you speak
        and say you are a blessin'?
Will they
        pay cold cash for
        a piece of you?
Do you
        have people workin' for you
        who all say how they love you? Oooo!

Are you a slick product
I can sink my chomps in?
Do you perform with intensity?
Are you a slick product
I can sink my chomps in?

Do you make thinkin' easy...
Do you make thinkin' easy...

Well, you've got all of the answers
        wrapped up in bow.
All of the answers wrapped up in a bow.
All of the answers wrapped up in a bow.
Do you make thinkin' easy for me?

Pelibre Latinx

Papi invents words in his delirium.
Angustanostra, which could mean our enjoyed sadness,
or Sarmolada, which sounds like an iconic, wintry peak named after a lost love.
But the one we cling to is Pelibre. Our eyes widen, "Oh,
that's a good one!" We think dangerous books but quickly realize the mistake:
it isn't peLIBRO. It's peLIBRE. Dangerous freedom.

Pelibre is the ability to study
in a country that is angry when you are at the head of the classroom.
Pelibre is dancing with precise anticipation of each beat, and
knowing someone will call you sleazy because you are comfortable with your body.
Pelibre is working 18 hour days as a revered, educated community leader,
only to have an ignorant person condescend to you because of your accent.

Pelibre is having the money and insurance to go to nearly any medical facility,
where the doctor looks at his laptop, not you, in order to check off all the drugs you need.
Pelibre is reading, speaking, and writing two or more languages fluently,
yet feeling ironically shunned in all the communities that your knowledge opens up to you.
Pelibre is claiming more than one country, memorizing the landscapes you love,
despite the fact that none of those lands claim you.

Pelibre is having the words and the inclination to state fire-
breathing truths, like Latinos/as were in the Americas before any walls were imagined.
Pelibre is grasping at more freedom and power and justice,
even when the consensus is that you barely deserve nutrition, or books, or dignity.
Pelibre is unabashed egotism, the shunning of sacrifice at the expense of soul,
a bold and supreme demand for awe at the spinning galaxy of talent and sympathy you offer,
when the world would place you upon the guillotine.

My father was pelibre.
My mother is pelibre.
One would assume I'm pelibre, by default.
No, my head is still hanging by its spinal cord.
I'm waiting, waiting for it to snap.

The Aliens

"The Attorney General may conduct any screening of such aliens that he deems appropriate, including screening to determine whether such aliens should be returned to their country of origin...." —From the Executive Order Regarding Undocumented Aliens in the Caribbean Region, The White House under President George W. Bush.

The aliens came in
as a vapor.
They were ancient beings,
very old,
some say immortal,
but others still insist
they never existed at all.
This is because
they are so small.
They floated through the universe,
hitching rides on comet tails
to pick up speed, if necessary.
Little viral microbes,
too miniscule
for most living things to notice.
They traveled long and far,
adapting themselves
to each new environment.
And this is how
they came to be
here.

Some of them were
left
in our upper atmosphere,
where they lingered for a long, long time.
A few came down,
gradually,
with rains and wind,
but they could easily find each other.
Their perception connection
was very strong.

Some said it was
telepathic,
others, again, refused to believe it.
When enough of them gathered
within our skies,
they decided to learn about us,
and this is when
the problem began.
For we humans couldn't see
the aliens,
even though we breathed them
into our bodies,
just like we might breathe in
any random vapor.

No one understood
what caused
the plague.
Panic ensued.
Pharmaceutical companies
worked through time
to create drugs
to attack the symptoms.
Soon, many efficient ones
were available
to anyone with money
to pay for them.
The injections were very popular.
They kept humans looking young
and healthy.
Folks were able to
remain active.
However,
the aliens were able to
mutate at will.
They were wise and strong,
thus able to live in almost any environment,
even one of attack.

So with each injection,
a new set of symptoms
kept cropping up.
Humans went mad
for the next set of injections,
anything to keep the alien symptoms
away.
They injected and injected,
until there were no satisfactory injections left,
and the ailing humans
died,
completely ravaged by their weak bodies.

But there was one girl
who felt differently.
On the evening when she inhaled
the aliens,
she thought she heard them speak
to her
in her sleep.

She heard them say they were there
to help her.
When she went to the government-mandated doctor
her poverty allowed,
with the first sign of symptoms,
she refused the injection.
The doctor insisted,
"The virus must be attacked, killed!"
She said that it couldn't be killed
and perhaps if it weren't attacked,
then it wouldn't counterattack
so fiercely.
The doctor called her insane.

She left and confined herself to a room.
News channels heard of
her theory and attempted to

interview her and debate the issue.
Her state of illness was carefully watched
around the world.
She began with digestive sickness
and dehydration.
She patiently drank water
with trembling lips.
Then the aliens challenged her
circulatory system and she
became very cold.
Her arteries, veins, capillaries
became filled with dead
white blood cells,
which seeped out of her skin
and crystallized into a beautiful, yellow
shell
that was built, layer upon layer,
like amber lace made of glass.
She took warm water
and painfully dissolved the shell,
slowly, every hour, without rest.
Some humans died during this stage,
falling asleep and becoming petrified
in a cast of topaz.
The aliens multiplied fiercely
in the dead body
and then escaped through the nose or mouth
they had entered,
to then find new hosts.

But the girl remained strong.
She allowed the aliens
to seize each organ, find its weakness,
and then move on to the next.
She coughed, moaned and cried out,
even though her voice gave.
The ordeal took her
six months,

after which she emerged
new.

Her body became their home.
The aliens had made her flesh
stronger.
She was now immune
to what killed so many weaker souls.

She began to find others
who had accepted the aliens
into their bodies.
They all opened a center
where the sick could come
and have help in becoming immune.
The pharmaceutical companies
and the Medical Association
attempted to shut down the center,
but found they could not
when it was proven that no one
dispensed drugs
or technical medical advice.
Slowly,
through time,
the aliens killed off all who attacked them
and made those who didn't
closer to being
immortal.

Pity Party
(a song to sing when encountering fascism)

Fascism's back in town again
Hands and knees on the ground again
Siren and cracked skull sounds again
At least we've got TV

Some went North quick that night, you know
Riddled with so much fright, you know
Some stayed and stand and fight, you know
Might they be better than me?

Cuz I'm
Completely miserable
Completely miserable
Completely miserable
Why don't you join me?

Some say practice self-care, that's right
Drink tea and sleep, there there, that's right
Do yoga, don't stay up all night
See friends to chat and eat

Others now pray all day, okay
Faith in good keeps the bad at bay
Don't get mad we've been had, they say
They say this ain't defeat

Then why am I
Completely miserable
Completely miserable
Completely miserable
Why don't you join me?
Livin' in misery....

(whispered)
Fascism's back in town again
Hands and knees on the ground again
Siren and cracked skull sounds again

(louder)
At least we've got TV
We've got corporate fascist TV
What's the damn point of news on TV
It's the same as an online screen
Or social media memes
We're all livin' in a psycho dream

(slower pace)
So I'm
Completely miserable
Completely miserable
Completely miserable
Why don't you join me?
We'll have our own private pity party!
Why don't you join me?!?!?!

The Grandparents I Will Never Meet

For Dr. Norma Elia Cantú

Papi's father died of tuberculosis when he was seven
he was a carpenter
I touched the small car and horse
he carved for my father, before he left the planet
the toys were smooth, as if Papi polished them with use
Mami says that Abuelo was known for his charm
it must be true, Papi being
a leader so charismatic, everyone in Logan Square flocked
his path, as he walked the neighborhood, smiling

> Mami's mother died of varying ailments, mainly her heart
> sadness ran in my family
> an aunt was said to have hung herself
> my grandmother carried the same grief, never smiling in photos
> Mami is the same way
> if a picture is taken, we have to tickle her for her to show her teeth

I have two images of my grandfather in Cuba
one is based on a photo that was kept in a magazine, carelessly thrown away
he is holding up a catch of several enormous fish, huge toothy grin
the second image is abuelo as a viejito, decaido, so wrinkled and skinny, toothless smile
these men refuse to converge in my mind, as if they were from different universes

> I wonder what I might have learned from
> their presence in my life, instead of
> esta mierda long distance or never-had-access-at-all
> existence with them: might have I become
> skilled at raising sails, or
> understood my mom's, my brothers', my own
> bouts of mental illness, or maybe
> might have Papi understood my artistic nature, if
> abuelo hadn't died, if I'd met any of them

I thought of this a long time when a mentor shared her birthday with me in Chicago, surrounded
by her family, sisters, nieces, cousins, all elaborating on things they'd cooked, sewn, built
together.

Women Wraiths

sages and journalists scribble scratch
claim we are a weightless vapor along the shore of a river
contemplating the sunset as the world forgets
what? the uterine mythology set in celluloid and cheap magazines?

pfffuu!

meanwhile, we dance a merengue with him/her who laps
our nectar off fingertips, sozzled in a stupor of joy
we wraiths screech into town on motorcycle growl and dust
bellow-laughing as the rest of you sit set in holy veils

but it's a-ight
you may not see our ebullience, but we see you
decades bring the delectable decadence of knowing all your biz-nizz
there is no gizmo preventing your ocular muscles from scoping the female form after 40
just admit it: you don't want to lock eyes because you don't want us to see you
the unseeable you, the sorrows, the illusions, the ways
you've failed, again and again

I find the irritation, the scar, the pearl
make a necklace of hueso and shells and raw insides
wear the creature 'round my neck

...at the gates...

Trash

Papi threw out all my artwork.

Derek's carved open chest,
blue-black heart and orange skin in
Design marker scrawl,
condemning our underground afternoon of
Southside sad lust.

A spotlighted box of cereal called "Health"
in a room with a grass floor, pine tree
decoration, and chopped lumber sitting neatly.
Acrylic nature. I miss this one the most.
I am reminded of it every time
I shop at Whole Foods.

Even the two-bits. Tiny 2x2 art,
entered in competition, or sold.
Two of mine won awards.
One of them, my first sale, was bought for $5.
It was a multi-colored, swirling
cathedral called "My Bed."

I placed all the work under the bed
in the guest room. By my next visit,
it was gone,

except for "Insane Bridget."
She is framed and in the living room,
face turned away, bony back
curved at the viewer, harsh
charcoal on brown paper.
Dark copper sadness, winner of a gold prize.

Papi values winning.
Anything else is trash.

And this is why, today, he is so afraid,
scared that retirement means he, too, is trash,

wary of children who might find him useless.

But artists make beauty out of trash.
We roll in the discarded and live with its decline,
listen to it crumble and make the sound song,
cradle it in our hands and sculpt it useful.

The Guts of a Corporation

when you have surgery
you must sign a form
agree to let the overseeing medical organization
dissect, reproduce, dilute
your removed organs into
anything
imagined by science

of course, you sign

under bright lights
under sedation
under the knife

you dream of:

you as an ear on a hamster
you as fat-free potato chips

you as Wilhemina Sotomayor, in 2035,
the first female WNBA star to beat a male NBA star in free throws

you as a baby who cannot grow beyond being a baby

you as a blond, green-eyed man who joins
an uber-Nazi organization, in 2076,
who celebrates 600 years of ignorance about his own cells,
chanting nonsense in a suburban park

you as a lump of red and purple flesh
screeching plooompsh ploompsh ploompsh all day
wheezing hnnnm hnnnm hnnnm hnnnm during lonely nights

you as a tiny, one millimeter cybernetic supercomputer
massaging electrons into unknown sounds
making the next movement of music to unite
the world with dance

you as biohazard garbage dumped into soil
becoming something woody, leafy, and tall

stretching into clouds
breathing under the same stars that, 3000 years
ago, saw you play, when you were something brown, something female

you as virus explosion, hurting
millions just by existing
you as vaccine, killing another
version of yourself, because
isn't that what growth is?

when you wake up, only you, the original, exist
except for the place in your belly that has been hollowed out

Pelota de Fuego (Ball of Fire)

I.

When Papi was a boy, in Barranquilla, Colombia,
he and his barrio friends could not afford a real fútbol,
so they tied a bunch of rags together and someone's mother smoothed
the strips into a soccer ball with her leg-pumped sewing machine.

Sometimes, they dipped the ball in tar, in order to make it even smoother—
Papi says it was like kicking around a lead ball, which explains his w-i-d-e calves.
Other times, before the tar dried, they lit it on fire
and kicked around their pelota de fuego through the dusty, already too-hot streets.

One particular priest did not like their antics and often scolded them,
which, of course, prompted them to kick la pelota de fuego right into his afternoon service.
The priest stumbled over it, kicked it out into the church yard,
where it set a pine tree aflame so quickly that the sparks from the tree
landed in between the breasts of a rotund church-goer who got up, screaming in a panic.

Mami says, "For this reason, we know that García-Márquez was not just inventing stories.
Those things really do happen in Latin America."

II.

Soccer games were a given at church outings:
picnics, camping trips, barbecues,
all had un juego de fútbol.

Papi was the minister and early for everything,
which gave me a dewy morning view of the players raising the nets and warming up.
That was all I watched, as I was more interested in swimming,
but I could hear them all day, screaming commands and the infamous "Gooool!"

At night, back home, my parents' room was somber.
Papi lay, face down, on his side of the bed.
Mami read her magazines next to him under dim yellow light.
"¿Que le pasa a papi?" I'd ask with eight year old concern.

"He thought he was 20 years old today."
After noticing my youthful confusion, she explained that people in their 40s can't play
fútbol all day in the sun. I thought, "How sad."

III.

Papi can't remember much anymore.

He recently forgot I was born in Chicago, stating, when I told him, "Oh, I never knew that."

The medication that minimizes these episodes sometimes gives him nightmares,

but on occasion, he has a great night.

He woke up one morning, during a visit, smiling.

"Soñe con fútbol," he said, after dreaming of playing soccer all night.

"Ai, es riiico jugar el fútbol," a corona of light around his face.

I am happy that in his dreams he can play fútbol all day again.

Chicago DJ Remix, North and Damen, 1993
(a song to sing for those of us who grew up in dance clubs and outlived everyone around us)
after Barbara Tucker's "Beautiful People"

deep
deep
deep
deep
Fiasco's drinkin' gin and tonic
deep
deep
deep
deep
Fiasco's drinkin' gin and tonic
deep
deep
deep
deep
curly girl's walkin' in with a fake fur
deep
deep
curly girl's walkin' in with a fake fur
deep
deep
blue...light in the water
deep
deep
red...light in the water
deep
deep
deep
deep
coat check girl is under eighteen
but her daddy's the owner, know what I mean
deep down
deep down
deep down
deep down

bartender is her brother
I ain't ever seen her mother
deep down
deep down
deep down
deep down
curly girl is spinnin' in the middle of the crowd
deep down
deep down
deep down
deep down
don't go into the stairwell
the walls and the floorboards have a thing or two to tell you
deep down
deep down
deep down
deep down
a sniff a pipe a sip a life
deep down
deep down
tick tock tick tock tick tock tick tock
deep down
deep down
deep down
deep down
slide that leg arms reach overhead
and bounce
deep down
and bounce
deep down
hide in a groove
in a circle that moves
deep down
in the wax
deep down
skippin' beats on the trax
deep down

in the wax
deep down
on the trax
deep down
deep down
deep down
curly girl is walkin' out as the loop ends
deep
deep
deep
deep
gatherin' in the alley
cars drivin' off to who? where?
deep
deep
deep
deep
good-bye
deep
deep
deep
deep
good-night

Textbook on the Desegregation of an Afro-Latinx

Chapter 1
the red flame flamboyán sitting on top of a Matanzas mountain
shelters the hesitant embrace of your light-skinned Mami and
negro Papi, open Caribbean Sea before them, ancient gateway, portal, key

Chapter 2
Abuelo boycotts the wedding porque Papi is too black
it will be 20 years before Mami speaks to Abuelito again
no one voices the silence at home, so you stay mute, too
quiet like a scroll wound so tight it cannot be opened to release its words

Chapter 3

you make books before you can read, stapled volumes of crayoned letters
Mami reads to you every night about Johnny Lion, the exploring cub
when you turn three, you read to her, and by five, you've written your first play
but your characters are like Snow White: foreign, cold, trapped

Chapter 4

Mozart School, in Logan Square, teaches you to be quiet is to die
so you better learn to yell and cuss and spit the evil eye, as if
you were two different people: the one who breaks a girl's glasses for kicking you and
the one who buys school supplies early and scores beyond her grade level on tests
someone quietly submits your name to a magnet school
you don't know who did that, but you take the tests and get in

Chapter 5

you are bussed to Kenwood Academy, where everyone is Black and
they see you as Black, so you go home and ask Mami, "Am I Black?"
Mami and Papi look at each other and say nothing, leaving you to
take algebra in 7th grade, and watch the rich African American
teenagers who drive to school in their parents' Rolls Royces or Jaguars and only
talk to kids who use Coach purses or wear clothes from Marshall Field's,
leaving you to wonder if you fit in with Logan's Latino/a wildcats or Hyde Park's Black
bourgeoisie

Chapter 6

you learn that the Kenwood college prep program was started to address
civil rights issues that were fought for in the 1960s, so you are proud,
excited to learn about your history, but your teachers only teach Thoreau,
Dickinson, the Greeks, the Holocaust, and you know this is good because
they say this is good, but you wonder about García Marquez, and Borges,
all the authors on Mami and Papi's bookshelves, and even more so you wonder about
Morrison, and Angelou and Hughes, who are also on Mami and Papi's bookshelves, and
you wonder why Kenwood is great at teaching you discipline and drive but isn't
teaching you about your Latinidad or what seems to be your emerging Blackness

Chapter 7

you stop paying much attention at school
instead you spend hours listening to Jello Biafra recite lyrics about Cambodian atrocities
RevCo frontman Al Jourgensen pounds beats into you about the Bhopal disaster
X-Ray Spex remind you that your identity does not lie in a false, gendered mirror
you resist the prevailing '80s message that greed is good, while classmates obsess over
gold hoops and getting into Ivy League schools and the latest Bell Biv Devoe
Mami and Papi fear you because you wear black boots and lipstick
and blue and purple bruises from slamdancing with shaved head Mexicanos from La Villita

Chapter 8

somehow you make it to college, you're even on the college newspaper, and you write
about how a catcalling man on the street said you didn't like him because he was Black, but
you answered, "I am Black," and he said, "You can only be a spic or something"
this idea seems wrong to you and you explain in your newspaper essay that
you identify as Black, you claim it, to all of Columbia College Chicago, in black and white print
a professor responds to the essay with a map of the Trans-Atlantic slave trade that shows
most Black slaves were transported to Cuba, Colombia, the Caribbean, South America, your
homes, your world is Black

Chapter 9

you go home and tell your parents, "I am clearly Black. Can you explain this to me? Tell me."
they slowly voice the story about Abuelo's racism, self-loathing, directed at their love
Mami explains how in her own family there are Black relatives, but they were ostracized, too
you are 22 years old when they finally tell you who you are
you have carried a black and white fissure, like marble stone, inside your stomach,
a rock you've instinctively tried to break with the pounding of flesh and bone under
black and white strobe lights, as if the answers were in the extremes
of dark and light, dark and light, dark and light

Chapter 10

you are almost 45, an educator of Latinx literature, Afro-Latinidad, la cultura tuya, but
the journey, you are certain now, began when you were bussed to Kenwood, and you saw
yourself in the Black faces of the proud, studious, driven-for-success peers surrounding you,
and they saw Black you, confused, at the edge of danger, and forgave you for not knowing
the separation had happened, for maybe they didn't know either, yet there you were, together
like siblings who had drifted off from sea wreckage, finally floating toward each other, ready
to begin a cuento that twists and turns like the salty writhing of a sparkling, multi-hued, crashing
wave with no beginningendseparation, an eternal spiral of knowledge as old as the gold fire in
the sky

Invisible Ink

I did not read my dad's death
certificate, too many bureaucratic lines,
fine print woven onto thick paper paid for
per copy. I shoved them in a folder, forgot
the moment we signed him into ash. Today,
I pulled the final forms out of a leopard
bag, noticed he was rendered white, like a ghost,
despite a mother whose grandfather was a Cacique,
father more Langston than Williams, Black
like ink seeping into tree pulp, a mishmash of fiber,
pressed carbon and the fear of squid. Erased,
a blank page, a deleted history typed in foreign characters.

Master of Academia

you've made me into such a pretty doll
you like me that way: stiff-
limbed like the immobilized unions
appeased with banging pots outside the high-rise
windows of leadership who hear nothing

refused to look at my shaved head, an affront to
the required subscription to gender radioactivity,
disintegrating my DNA into long hair hedges and the many, "Oh!
Can you explain that to me?" and "I agree with [fill in white colleague's name here]"
sentences like a feminized torture made of hands, feet, and eyes
bound with the pages of a canon that renders me invisible

silenced my language into a cohort of students in the permanent
purgatory of perpetual remediation, forcing them to write
stories that center the exported version of your white
supremacy and how it tore off their own doll legs at the border,
all so you can say, "How sad," and remind them of the difference between
"run" and "ran," making sure the battery in my own back is kept on low
and the string you pull mimics your own voice

placed a filter in front of my image that whitens
my appearance, straightens my doll hair, renders me into a bland
soup without flavor, like a classroom discussion devoid of application,
meaning and context, obscuring the paths Black and Brown scholars need,
or like the vapid creation of a committee to address the need for a committee
formed to address the statistics that show that Afro-Latinx professors
cannot move into dead muñeca leadership positions on committees in their departments

despite tenure, I am an adjunct, a non-essential part, an accessory
ready to be dismissed by the child who grew bored with its toy,
tossed into a life without healthcare, certainty, or dinner
parties put on administrator's expense accounts, held under rotundas
built brick-by-brick by our students' ancestors who are forgotten by you
and them, because all of the statues on campus teach them nothing about themselves

see the doll you created, or don't see it, it is your choice, your whim

meanwhile, I have started a bonfire
set myself ablaze
parts are burning
smoke is rising

facades are there to mask reality
you never saw me coming

...the end that is no end...

New Year's Eve, New Orleans Restaurant, 2019-2020

what was meant to be an escape from death
my father's, my aunt's, my uncle's, my husband's uncle
all in one year, now it, too, nearly gone

I barely lifted my fork halfway to my mouth before he dropped
an elderly man with a heart condition
the room widened like the aperture of a camera, tables cleared, folks stood in a circle

no one ate as they pressed the defibrillator down on his chest
we just looked at each other, mouths closed, mum
I held my lover's hand

trained EMTs worked quickly to revive him, I don't know if they did
once he was gone, the restaurant staff apologized to us
some patrons left without paying or complained about the nuisance

we prayed, thanked the universe for this moment
tables were returned to the center of the room, as if to close the all-seeing eye
new revelers came in and feasted without any knowledge of what had happened

later, we walked arm in arm, city lit in gold and crimson
stopped at a corner where a brass band wailed, so we
danced and danced, fully aware of the ruin all around us

It takes a pandemic...

...to remember the dark
shadows on the flimsy cardboard walls of a house
creaking in a rainstorm, the six of us huddled,
telling stories in Spanish under melting wax
light, giggling because we were dry and fed and safe

...to consider the boy whose bed was on fire
because his mother lit it "in one of her fits,"
he said, outside of the McDonald's, hungry, waiting
like me, to return to the half-way home, part of us
wanting shelter, part of us wanting to stay cold and free

...to devour the sacs inside the sliced mandarin,
hunger for a sweet you carelessly tossed into grey garbage
cans as a kid, oblivious to the bulb ready to run electric, matter
made elixir, a mood-altering onslaught of que se yo que, like
a river of nourishment that currently runs to you, but didn't always.

We are Not All in the Same Quarantine

one of my students, a young man with a sweet voice
was homeless, alone, before COVID-19 hit
he emailed me—from where? an overcrowded shelter?
—to let me know CUNY was trying to get him a laptop
so he could finish the work in my class, please don't worry
I told him, you'll get a good grade regardless

an influencer who fell ill texted a friend doctor
who conjured a test for the virus within 24 hours
she moved to her Hamptons home after learning she was positive
Instagrammed "getting fresh air" on Long Island
apologized when she was criticized for her privilege, access to tests
thousands cannot get, Nordstrom dropped its deal with her

we are not all in the same quarantine

a friend in a tiny 12X12 apartment in Times Square
had a Zoom birthday party where she got drunk and
talked about *Tiger King* and *A Streetcar Named Desire*
a partygoer played "Get Lucky" and we all sat-danced to
"we've come too far to give up who we are"
and for a moment we all laughed with each other

Stacyann Chinn posts her indoor workouts with her daughter
who is about eight years old, full of joy, a tiny figure with fluffy hair
they giggle and slide around the living room in mismatched socks
talk about the universe, science, art, and Stacyann explained
not all kids get along with their parents, some parents hit their kids
her daughter's face went solemn, confused, and she asked, "But why?"

we are not all in the same quarantine

introverts have tea, choose a book from extensive collections
placed along the full length of a wall, listen to records on vinyl
play with their cat, who is snuggled next to the radiator
tinkling rain falling on the pane outside the window
groceries are delivered from Imperfect Foods, placed on the porch
the only time the introverts step outside

Amazon employees take pictures of garbage under storage shelves
in the warehouse, complain on Twitter that they don't have protection
such as gloves, masks, or sanitizer to prevent infection
and then the on-site outbreaks begin, other workers get sick
some die, and then the protest: employees walk out
meanwhile, some of us still order "essential" items, like ping pong tables

we are not all in the same quarantine

thousands of migrant workers in India are forced to stop working
told to travel back to their home, meaning "leave the country"
at the border they are told they might have the disease, so go back
they must, walk hundreds of miles to migrant camps without
water, soap, food, or any means of life or education for their children
no one has a plan for those who might get sick in the crowded quarters

meanwhile countries like South Korea and Iceland tested everyone
hired detectives to find people who might have come in contact with the virus
paid workers who must be in quarantine, delivered food to the sick
kept the outbreak numbers low and their economies in tact
yet, our own leaders question if our sick actually need ventilators, refuse to
test widely, remind everyone, we've done a great job, we've done a great job, we're so great

we are not all in the same quarantine

Ways of Seeing My Brothers

Uno
You are precise artisans, designing aircrafts meant to soar above the altocumulus,
or pumping air pulsating through twists of brass trumpet, pressing fingers down on
valves to scream higher than a jet.

Dos
Smirking boys in a 70s photograph, unaware of the holes in your socks.

Tres
Fearless little men, walking into classrooms filled with children who will only think to ask,
"Are you a spic?"

Cuatro
        I do not see you in jail the night you totaled Mami's car
        I do not see you stoned or geeked out, lonely and alienated in the college dorm
        I do not see you terrified when you see no options in the want ads
        I do not see you when you cry alone when your best friend fell in a rain of bullets
        I only see the miraculous feat of survival, how you managed the impossible:
        staying alive when the world told you every day you did not exist

Cinco
I remember the day your daughter was born, dear brother, and you had to fill out a form, choose Black
or White. Your oblivious white wife saw the X by the word Black and asked you why and you said, "Well
I sure as hell ain't white," and all of a sudden you gave
your own kind of birth.

Seis
I wore your clothes, walked like what we call a boy, talked knucklehead
talk, became what you were.

Siete

The only time I met Tio Segundo en Cuba, who built his home with black market wood, his dirty work-man jeans the same as the ones I saw on you, brother, after a day of roofing, and my heart hurt because I knew the two of you needed each other, drank yourselves into oblivion because you longed for each other, yet you would never meet.

Ocho

I listened at your doors   Devo   bang bang bang

Santana   Black magic

sat for hours

wondered in AC/DC electric

curiosity fizzling like

guitar feedback

waited for you

to open the passageway

Nueve

are you safe, dear brothers?
I cannot protect you from this
obsession with your demise
all I can offer is what I have seen
remember, what I see is beauty

Things to Pack on the Way to Everywhere

scent of a morning Weymouth pine
forest that huddled under lightning
storms at the midnight hour

                                palo santo, shea butter, both surprise gifts from a friend

        one speckled igneous rock
        your mother painted with clear polish
        "son lindos cuando brillan"

                                         unseen prism hues in dew

apricot after-glow of sunset
resting on your father's face de canela

                three nibbled acorns
                carelessly discarded
                items by the precocious periwinkle hare

                        a gold goblet of bitter wine

           Neneh Cherry's
           fuck-off pose

recetas de abuela: bollo de yuca y arroz con leche

                           the melancholy of the
                           Long-Eared owl's hoo hoo hoo

   a blue towel of Turkish cotton

           the TWHAK of drunk
           slapping a surprised abuser

pens in blue and green

                                        a scroll made of linen and embers

prayer cards to the holy trinity of AOC, SCOTUS Justice Sotomayor, La Lupe

                        Rita's anemone

homemade marshmallows
teriyaki beef jerky   a carving of my lover's eyelashes
organic raisins and jumbo cashews

                                tears of a rooster five minutes before dawn
                                Cuban or Puerto Rican, no importa, son los mismos

                two wax candles
                a phallus, a vulva
                made by an androgynous Palenquerx
                anointed by heliconius butterflies
                reminding us mimicry is the tool of saints

Jesse De La Peña's
Chicago scratch

                                one chartreuse paint chip
                                scratched off a rusty sign in San Antonio

                a lick of cold gin
                slid off a New Jersey ice
                luge while a flannelled comedian sings
                stories to his dream-deferred cousins at 4 am

                                        Camphor lip balm
                                        matches

the bag will be small, light
contain unseen subuniverses
that, on occasion, will emit their own
luminescence

Words of Thanks

First and foremost, I have to thank poet/playwright/educator Vincent Toro, my partner in life, for always believing in my work and in me, and inspiring me with his own cosmic creativity. Thank you for your countless hours of feedback, humor, and love. There is nothing more precious than what we share between us.

Secondly, I must thank Roberto Carlos Garcia, my editor, for understanding my subversive and bizarre vision. Such folks are rare and I am so grateful to be under the kind wing of the Get Fresh family. Thank you for creating a publishing house that amplifies the voice of so many talented poets who share their own unique brand of beauty—they are all my brothers and sisters, now, and how lucky am I for that?

I would also like to thank (in no particular order): Editor and Founder Laura Pegram at *Kweli Journal*; Poetry Editor Nicole Terez Dutton at *The Baffler*; Emma Trelles, editor of *MiPoesias* and guest editor at *Best American Poetry* blog; Francisco Aragón, guest editor at *Best American Poetry* blog and founder of the Andrés Montoya Poetry Prize at The University of Notre Dame; Editor Raina León and Guest Editor Peggy Robles Acevedo at *Acentos Journal*; Editors Bettina Love and Venus Evans-Winters; Editor Danny Shot at *Red Fez*; Editor Chavisa Woods (and posthumously, Founder Steve Cannon) at *Gathering of the Tribes*; Dr. Norma Cantú, editor at the Society for the Study of Gloria Anzaldúa and guest editor at *American Studies Journal*; Editor Maria Mazziotti Gillan at *Paterson Literary Review*; Editor/Producer/Director Summer Dawn Reyes at *In Full Color*; Editor and Producer Cindy Cooper at *Reproductive Freedom*; Jennifer Juneau and Linda Kleinbub at Black and White Bar's *Fahrenheit Around the World*; City Lore and Bowery Arts + Science and Roni Schotter; Creative Writing Editor Patricia Trujillo at *Chicana/Latina Studies*; Poetry Editor Jim LaVilla-Havelin at *The San Antonio Express News*; Guest Editor Liliana Wendorff at *Pembroke Magazine*; Editors Matt Goodwin, Alex Hernandez, and Sarah Rafael García at the Latinx Archive project; Editor Lisa Alvarado; and The Tattoosday Project. Thank you so much for supporting my work and for the community you have provided. I am humbled by the beautiful work that you do. Thanks in particular to Rachel Eliza Griffiths, Yesenia Montilla, and Willie Perdomo, for your generous support. Also many thanks to Victoria Russell, Ysabel Y. Gonzalez, and Martin Farawell at the Geraldine Dodge Poetry Program, and all the Macondistas who have supported me at the Macondo Foundation.

Finally, my dear friends who continue to remind me that I, indeed, do exist and that my voice has a place in this world—thank you (in no particular order): Marina Carreira and Cindy Goncalves; Nancy Mercado; Ellen Hagan and David Flores; Diana Díaz; Papoleto; Nova and Alyssa Gutierrez and Family; The Del Cid Family; Bobby DeJesus; Cynthia Tobar; JP Howard, Cynthia Manick, and Women Writers in Bloom; Jenny Saldaña; Barbara Wrightson; Chris Ludecke; Teresa Veramendi and J. Michael Martinez; Nomie Pace Wallace and Family; Carmen Rivera Tirado and Candido Tirado; Cliff Morehead and Family; Dimitri Reyes; Nick Merchant; Andrew DiClemente; Gerard Briones; Greg Segarra; Mwalim; Tim Breitberg; Jen Lazo; all the First Spanish Crew; Bill and Rachel Rood; Marina Gutierrez; Fred Wood; Da'non Bolden; Cherria

Morrow (wherever you are); Vernon Robinson; Michael VanCalbergh, Bryanna Lee, and family; Tachelle Wilkes; Carolina Hinojosa-Cisneros; Kim "Evolution" Crawley; Christine Goodman; Dr. Sonja Lanehart; Oscar Bermeo; Anthony M. Flores (and San Antos Poetry Scene); Rick Villar; Fish Vargas; Beluvid Ola-Jendai; Nancy Mendez-Booth; All the Latina Outsiders; Andy Powell and Julia Berick; the Chicago Club Naked/Red Dog Crew; Rodney and Dava (The Peace Posse); Urayoán Noel; Onome Om; Melissa Coss Aquino; Kamilah Aisha Moon; Edwin Roman; Rosebud Ben-Oni; Ching-In Chen and Cassie Mira; Wendy Call; Kristen Millares-Young; Renee Watson; Marcos De La Fuente; Toni M. Kirkpatrick; Emari DiGiorgio; Terry and Elly Simon; the late Robert Waddell; The BCC Association of Latino Faculty and Staff Family; Sandra Maria Esteves; Gloria Rodriguez; Bridget Bartolini and the Five Boro Story Project; Denice Frohman; Noel Mendez; Raquel Salas Rivera; Karen Jaime; Dr. Wendy Barker; Dr. Monique Guishard; The DreamYard Crew; The Kenwood Crew; The CUNY/BCC Crew; The Acosta Family (worldwide); The Ceballos Family (en Cuba); The Toro Family; and my dear students. All of you have supported my work in some way and/or shown me kindness and community when I needed it on my poetic journey. Thank you so much for noticing and celebrating with me as we walk toward the horizon.

DR. GRISEL Y. ACOSTA is an associate professor at the City University of New York-BCC. She is the editor of the Routledge anthology, *Latina Outsiders Remaking Latina Identity*. Her first book of poetry, *Things to Pack on the Way to Everywhere*, is a finalist for the 2020 Andrés Montoya Poetry Prize, and forthcoming in 2021, from Get Fresh Books. She is also a contributor to many other anthologies and journals including, but not limited to: *Celebrating Twenty Years of Girlhood: The Lauryn Hill Reader*; *African American Women's Language*; *The Routledge Companion to Latino/a Literature*; *Check the Rhyme: An Anthology of Female Poets and Emcees*; *In Full Color: The First Five Years Anthology*; and *Short Plays on Reproductive Freedom*. Her work can also be found in *Best American Poetry*, *The Baffler*, *Kweli Journal*, *Red Fez*, *Gathering of the Tribes*, *Acentos Journal*, *Vida: Women in Literary Arts*, and *Salon*. She is a Geraldine Dodge Foundation Poet and a Macondo Fellow.